Portrait of
MOURNE

SIMON WATTERSON

HALSGROVE

First published in Great Britain in 2010

Copyright © Simon Watterson 2010
The author asserts his moral rights.

British Library Cataloguing-in-Publication Data
A CIP record for this title is available from the British Library

ISBN 978 1 84114 844 1

HALSGROVE
Halsgrove House,
Ryelands Industrial Estate,
Bagley Road, Wellington, Somerset TA21 9PZ
Tel: 01823 653777   Fax: 01823 216796
email: sales@halsgrove.com

Part of the Halsgrove group of companies
Information on all Halsgrove titles is available at: www.halsgrove.com

Printed and bound in China by Toppan Leefung Printing Ltd

INTRODUCTION

"The Mournes", what does this mean to you? Perhaps it's day trips to Newcastle or walking on the sandhills at Murlough; maybe it's family holidays in Tollymore or looking down on the shimmering expanse of the Silent Valley from Slieve Binnian. These might be typical responses from the visitor to Mourne, but there are also those for whom the area is their home and the source of their livelihood – farmers and fishing communities whose lives may be tied to the land and the sea through generations. However, it might surprise many people to learn that perhaps no other area in the northeast of Ireland holds greater significance to Ulster than Mourne – a bold claim surely, but one with merit. We'll come back to that later. But first, where is Mourne and what are the Mournes?

The name Mourne comes from a tribe called the Mughdhorna who, around AD 1150, came from what are the modern-day counties of Monaghan and Louth to settle in the low plain on the northern side of Carlingford Lough. Their new kingdom was protected by the sea to the south and by the mountains to the north. At that time the mountains themselves were known by a different name, *Na Beanna Boirche*, and it is only more recently that they have come to be known as the Mountains of Mourne, or simply the Mournes. In turn, the mountains have passed the name on to the rolling countryside to their north and west. Modern day Mourne is a much larger area than the small area occupied by the Mughdhorna and this book looks at the current Mourne Area of Outstanding Natural Beauty (AONB). The Mourne AONB designation is well deserved; the area is truly beautiful. It is also an area of great contrasts: the high peaks and the low plains; glorious sunshine and plentiful rain; golden beaches and shaded forests; but everywhere some form of beauty for those prepared to find it.

The heart of modern day Mourne is surely the High Mournes. These are a ring of 12 granite peaks that cluster near Slieve Donard, which at 850m is the highest mountain in the Mournes. They were formed when a large underground block of shale collapsed and the space was filled with upwelling magma, which then cooled to form granite. The remaining shale roof was scraped away by glacial ice exposing this granite heart. The Western Mournes were formed in a similar way but, in contrast to the pyramidal peaks of the High

Mournes, they rarely rise above 600m. Further to the west again, the hills subside into low, shale-covered foothills and then into the drumlins of the Newry lowlands. To the south of the mountains lies the low Kilkeel plain, subdivided into a patchwork of small fields by drystone walls made of stones dug out from the fields themselves. Down on the shore, wrack beds were used as a source of fertiliser for the fields while the sea itself was a source of food and a trade route. Some of this trade was illicit in nature and smuggled goods were moved through the mountains via the Brandy Pad to places like Hilltown. On this side of the mountains the rolling countryside is mostly farmland dotted with small townlands and a few larger market towns such as Castlewellan. Nearby Newcastle is the main tourist hub for Mourne. This is one of the sunniest and driest places in Northern Ireland and when the town was linked to Belfast by the (now disused) Belfast and County Down Railway, it became a popular holiday destination … and it still is.

In contrast to the good weather of the coast, the mountains have some of the heaviest rainfall in the country. The natural storage and slow release of this water by the peat covering gives a clue to the reason why the mountains are of such importance to the wider region. The rapidly expanding industrialised Belfast of the early twentieth century required ever increasing amounts of water. The threat of water shortages resulted in the formation of a commission to identify and secure adequate water supplies. The commission looked at a number of sites but the extraordinary purity of Mourne water combined with the high rainfall made the area ideally suited. The result was the Silent Valley reservoir, the Ben Crom reservoir and a tunnel under Slieve Binnian to collect the waters of the Annalong Valley – capable of supplying 130 million litres of water per day. The 22-mile Mourne Wall, a unique feature of the Mournes linking the summits of 15 mountains, was built over an eighteen-year period to delimit the 9000-acre catchment area for the reservoirs. The water collected in these reservoirs enabled the continued operation and expansion of the linen, shipbuilding and other industries in the city of Belfast. Today, although the industry has mostly gone, 400,000 people rely on the water from the Mournes.

For me, Mourne is all about the forests and hills, the rolling countryside and the splashing streams. Approached with patience and humility, Mourne reveals a little more of itself to me on every visit but, rain or shine, the undeniable beauty of Mourne is a constant. This beauty is what keeps me coming back. As you turn the pages of this book and see the dawn light on Slieve Bearnagh, the riot of autumn colours in Tollymore, or the waters of the Silent Valley that could end up in your kettle, ask yourself again, what do the Mournes mean to you?

River Lagan

BALLYNAHINCH

Finnis

BANBRIDGE

River Bann

Slieve Croob

Mourne wall

AONB Boundary

Castlewellan
Forest Park

Lough Island
Reavy

Dundrum

Castlewellan

Tollymore
Forest Park

Hilltown

NEWCASTLE

Slieve
Bearnagh

Slieve
Donard

Spelga Dam

Bloody Bridge

Slieve
Binnian

Eagle
Mountain

Attical

Annalong

WARRENPOINT

Rostrevor

KILKEEL

Greencastle

The Shimna is the loveliest of the rivers that flow through Mourne,
whether clothed in the golden colours of autumn …

… or the cool, shaded greens of summer.

The trees reflected in the perfect mirror of the Mountain Lake in Castlewellan Forest Park givesan impression of what the lakes of the High Mournes might have looked like before their deforestation.

The Glen River flows down through Donard Forest to the sea at Newcastle. This is one of the popular routes to the summit of Slieve Donard.

Beech, oak, alder and birch: the fallen leaves of these trees cling to the wet rock of a small stream.

Right: The wind whips the branches of a riverside walk in Tollymore as the autumn leaves carpet the ground.

The Ice House was constructed some time around the 1840s to store food and provide ice for the Annesley Estate.

Right: The sea washes the feet of the Mournes in the warm glow of the pre-dawn light.

The Meeting of the Waters – the Spinkwee River, which rises on the slopes of
Slievenaglogh and Slieve Commedagh, meets the Shimna in Tollymore.

The riverbed of the Spinkwee River – the water that runs off the hills
is so pure that it can be like looking through glass.

Slieve Binnian and Ben Crom frame the rounded bulk of Slievenaglogh
as the mid-winter sun sets behind the mountains.

There is a long history of wild-camping in the mountains. Care for the land and respect for the landowners are a small and worthwhile price for the privilege.

The rivers of Mourne run in spate during the winter.

Right: Looking north towards Castlewellan, with Slieve Croob peeking out from a covering of cloud.

The classic view of the High Mournes from the north.

The Shimna is at times peaceful…

...and sometimes turbulent as it churns and foams with the
autumn rain carrying the fallen leaves of oak and beech downstream.

View from the Shelter Stone – there are several shelter stones located throughout the mountains.
This one, consisting of several large slabs of granite, under which refuge from the
weather can be taken, looks out over the Ben Crom reservoir.

Ben Crom looms over the dam that holds back the waters of the Ben Crom reservoir.

Built to demarcate the Mourne water catchment area, the Mourne Wall is one of the defining features of the mountains. It is 22 miles long, passes over 15 summits and took eighteen years to build. It is a testament to the skill and hard work of the men who built it, but in certain places the mountains assert their own authority.

Surviving in the Mournes can be tough, but life is persistent
and finds a foothold in the most unlikely of places.

The Mountains of Mourne are known around the world thanks to the Percy French song in which he describes how they "...sweep down to the sea". Here Slieve Donard, Thomas's Mountain and Millstone Mountain can be seen sweeping down to the sea reflected in a sculpture in Newcastle.

In contrast to the exposed granite of the mountains, the rock that
originally covered them can be seen down on the shore.

Granite quarrying was one of the main industries in Mourne along with farming and fishing. Mourne granite kerbstones were used on the streets of Belfast, Liverpool, Manchester, Birmingham and London.

Quarrying has left its scars on the mountains, but even here beauty can be found.

Wood sorrel is abundant throughout the forests and woods of Mourne. It can be eaten sparingly and is sometimes referred to as shamrock, although traditional shamrock is actually three-leafed old white clover.

Bell heather and ling grow side-by-side throughout the summer months and give the brown hills some welcome colour.

Trees shade the Mountain Lake from the early summer sun.

Tollymore Forest Park was the former demesne of the Roden family, who sold it in two parts to the Department of Agriculture in the 1930s and '40s. It has a wealth of tree species, some indigenous and some imported. Timber from Tollymore was used for the interior of the *Titanic*.

Slievenaslat is a modest peak, but it is hidden in the trees above Castlewellan and is a beautiful, quiet place from which to admire the mountains.

Left: The land around Castlewellan was granted to the Annesleys in 1742. In 1856 the 4th Earl had the current castle constructed in the Scottish baronial style.

Right: The lake at Castlewellan is nearly a mile long and is a popular spot for canoeing and fishing. It also hosts the Irish University Rowing Championships.

The old church at Maghera is a site of great antiquity. It was important because it was on the main route from Newry to Downpatrick. Its name comes from *machaire ratha*, the plain of the fort.

The round tower at Maghera was probably between 26 and 29
metres tall before it was blown down around 1711. It was one of four ecclesiastical towers
in County Down, the others being at Nendrum, Drumbo and Downpatrick.

Clough Castle is an Anglo-Norman motte-and-bailey. Not much is known
of its history but it is believed it was an outpost of Dundrum Castle.

Right: There has been a keep on the site of Narrow Water Castle since 1212. It was built to prevent
attacks on Newry via the river. The current keep is a fine example of a sixteenth-century Irish tower house.

Sheep farming is an important part of the economy in Mourne.

Right: Traditional houses in Mourne were built to blend in with the landscape, nestling in against the hills to protect them from prevailing winds.

The sun sets behind the *Liagán Áine* – the Pillar of Enya. Enya was a mythical goddess beloved by Finn McCool, but despite being named after her, the Legananny Dolmen is actually a Neolithic portal tomb.

Top right: Drumena Cashel is a stone farmstead from the early Christian period. The opening in the ground is the entrance to the souterrain that would have been used for the storage of food.

Bottom right: Binder's Cove (also known as the Finnis Souterrain), is a superb example of the underground tunnels that were common in the early Christian period. The main passage is 30 metres long with two 6-metre side passages. It was most probably used for safe storage, but may also have been used as a refuge during times of attack.

The River Lagan, which flows through Belfast, arises on the slopes of Slieve Croob.
Here it passes through Finnis at the foot of the mountain.

Bluebells in Castlewellan – this is one of the best places to see this wonderful annual display of colour.

Light filters through the leaf of an acer tree in the Annesley Garden.

Left: The 100-acre National Arboretum in Castlewellan, with the walled Annesley Garden at its centre, is the finest in Ireland.

Looking up into the tree canopy.

The Peace Maze in Castlewellan, constructed between 2000 and 2001, has a path of 2 miles and covers 2.7 acres. Until 2007 it held the record for being the longest permanent hedge maze in the world.

The Belfast and County Down Railway built the Slieve Donard Hotel at the end of the nineteenth century as a luxury hotel for guests arriving by train. The railway link from Belfast to Newcastle played a major role in making Newcastle a popular holiday destination.

Lough Island Reavy was constructed between 1837 and 1839 to ensure a regulated water supply for the linen mills in the Bann Valley. At 250 acres, a top level of 40 feet and a capacity of 1400 million gallons of water, it held fifteen weeks supply at the height of the linen boom.

The Annalong Valley – Slievelamagan, Cove Mountain, Slieve Beg, Slieve Commedagh, Slieve Donard, Rocky Mountain and Chimney Rock Mountain.

Left: Slievelamagan, with the Blue Lough at its foot and the Ben Crom reservoir on its western flank. The name, from *Sliabh Lámhagáin*, means "creeping mountain" because its steepness meant it had to be ascended on all fours.

The Ben Crom reservoir takes its name from the craggy Ben Crom that looms over the water.

The oddly titled Percy Bysshe, presumably named after the poet.
It is a popular place for novice climbers and there is a narrow cave underneath it.

Right: The Spelga Dam was built
to catch the waters of the River
Bann, which arises on the
slopes of Slieve Muck.

The shelter on Slieve Commedagh – the Mourne Wall does not visit the nearby summit of this mountain, which is marked by one of the High Cairns.

The Summit Cairn of Slieve Commedagh and the Great Cairn on Slieve Donard are two of only 24 surviving early-to-middle Bronze Age cairns in County Down. Walkers could be excused for thinking they are merely summit markers, but both these High Cairns are burial cairns.

The Annals of the Four Masters records that in Anno Mundi 2533 "Slainge, son of Partholan, died in this year, and was interred in the cairn of Sliabh Slangha." The mountain was later renamed Slieve Donard after Saint Domangart. The cairn has been substantially damaged over the years.

The reflection of a bridge in the waters of the Fonfanny reservoir. The Foffany Dam water treatment works provides up to 52 millions litre of water a day to 100,000 people in the South Down area.

Trees are reflected in the gentle waters of the Mill Pond in Tollymore.

The Mourne Way runs for 26 miles from Newcastle to Rostrevor and is also part of the Ulster Way.

Right: Viewed from the West Tor of Hen Mountain, the Mourne Way wends it way beside Rocky River with the bulk of Eagle Mountain and Shanlieve in the background.

The Mourne Way, follows mixed terrain: sometimes forest, sometimes open hillside, but always a chance to get your feet wet.

The early morning sun casts a bright warmth over the yellow gorse, purple heather and the lower slopes of Slievenabrock and Luke's Mountain.

Hare's Gap, the col between Slievenaglogh and Slieve Bearnagh
is one of the most popular routes into the High Mournes.

The Mountains of Mourne sweep down
to the sea at Carlingford Lough.

Right: Looking across Mill Bay to the most
southerly of the Western Mournes.

The sandhills at Murlough were the centre of early human habitation in Mourne and a large collection of flint tools, pottery and jewellery has been found there. It is also a rich habitat for plants – Robert Lloyd Praeger, the great Irish naturalist, collected 250 plant species in just two days from the Murlough area.

The Mountains of Mourne from Murlough. One of the most distinctive features of the Mournes is that the visitor can see the full height of the mountains from sea to summit.

The Mountains of Mourne viewed from the south.

Black guillemots at Annalong Harbour – the old stone walls of the harbour
are an important breeding ground for this charming bird.

Dragonflies need still water in which to lay their eggs and
the mountains and valleys in Mourne are not short of ideal pools.
This keeled skimmer is one of the rarer dragonflies that
can be found in the Mournes.

The High Mournes and Western Mournes are split by a single road that provides the only access to Kilkeel other than via the narrow strip of coast at each mountain foot.

74

The viewpoint at Curraghard looks out over Newcastle and Dundrum Bay as the sun rises on an autumn morning.

The farmland of the Kilkeel plain extends right up to the foothills of Slieve Binnian.

Right: These red (now faded) gates are a common sight throughout the Mournes. This was the colour of choice for the Belfast Water Commissioners and the red gates appear wherever access was needed, especially along the route of old Mourne conduit that carried water to Belfast.

Looking across the southern flank of Pigeon Rock Mountain towards the High Mournes
where they meet the Kilkeel plain – this is part of the old Kingdom of Mourne.

Right: The Kilkeel plain is covered in a neat patchwork of fields.

The Ben Crom reservoir was constructed in the 1950s to meet the increasing demands for water from Belfast and County Down. In contrast to the earth and rock of the dam across the Silent Valley, this dam was constructed using concrete – it took 186 men three years to complete.

The Bloody Bridge is far more beautiful than its name suggests. It is named after an alleged massacre of prisoners being transported from Newry to Newcastle.

Shan Slieve lies just to the north of Slieve Commedagh and overlooks the Pot of Pulgarve.

The setting sun casts its last warm rays on the granite West Tor of Hen Mountain.

For many people Doan is the centre of the Mournes – it provides
wonderful views of the both the High and Western Mournes.

Right: Doan's name comes from *Dún Maol Chobha* – "Maol Chobha's fort",
although there is no record or evidence for an actual fort on the mountain.

The Silent Valley reservoir – it took 2,000 workmen ten years to complete the construction of the rock and mud dam that would hold back the waters of the Kilkeel River. Before the construction of the dam, the valley was known as the Happy Valley – the hills would echo the songs of the Cornish miners looking for tin.

86

The overflow water from the Silent Valley reservoir passes this elegant ship-like structure.

The summit of Eagle Mountain; at 638m it is the highest of the Western Mournes.

Full moon over the Blue Lough, cupped between Slievelamagan and Slieve Binnian.

Looking out over the Western Mournes in the golden light just before the sun sets.

Dawn on Slieve Bearnagh viewed from the North Tor.

The fields in Mourne are divided by dry-stone walls, which are
made from rocks dug out from the fields themselves.
The open structure allows the (sometimes fierce)
winds to pass through without damaging the walls.

Left: Looking down the Mourne Wall to the
North Tor of Bearnagh.

Slieve Meelbeg, Slieve Meelmore and Slieve Bearnagh from Doan.

Left: Lough Shannagh – the lake of the foxes. This beach-fringed lake is a popular place for wild swimming but legend recalls the death of the daughter of the local clan leader who pursued a fox into the lake only to be swallowed by the waters.

The Mourne Wall and the Western Mournes from Slieve Loughshannagh.

Right: The High Mournes from the summit of Slieve Loughshannagh.

The Mourne Wall traverses the summits of Slieve Meelmore,
Slieve Meelbeg and Slieve Loughshannagh.

Left: Dawn over Slieve Commedagh and Slieve Donard
from the North Tor of Bearnagh.

The Summit Tor of Slieve Bearnagh in the warm evening sun.

Right: Sunset over Slieve Meelbeg from
the summit of Slieve Bearnagh.

Approaching Hare's Gap from Slieve Bearnagh.

A walker stands on the summit of Slieve Bearnagh in the late evening sunshine.

The Trassey Track, overlooked by Spellack to the south.

Right: The Devil's Coachroad splits the face of Slieve Beg and provides the more adventurous walker with a route to the head of the Annalong Valley.

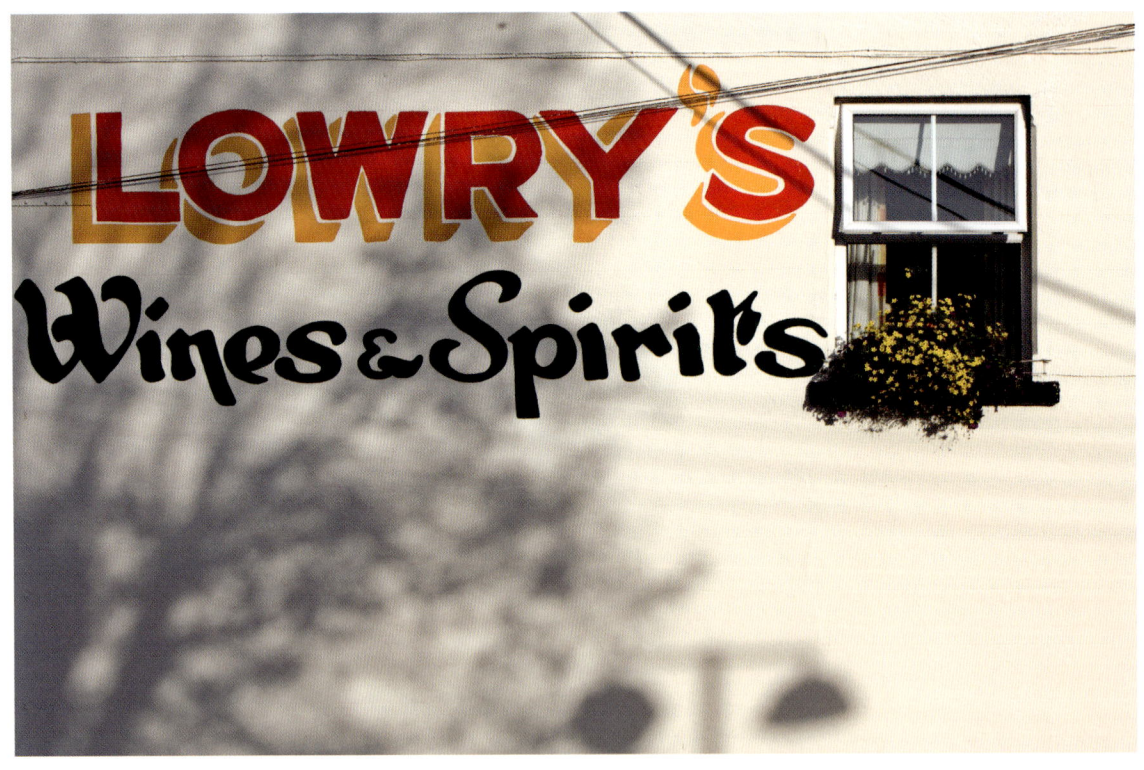

In 1835 there were 21 houses in Hilltown and 10 of these were public houses.
This was largely due to the trade in smuggled alcohol coming along the Brandy Pad from the coast.

The Brandy Pad is the infamous smuggling route through the mountains. Goods
such as alcohol, tobacco and silks were landed along the coast near to the Bloody Bridge
and then carried through the mountains to avoid the scrutiny of the Customs men.

The Mourne Mountain Marathon is the
oldest organised outdoor event in the Mournes
– the 2009 event was the 30th year.

Left: Looking down into the Pot of Legawherry from the
col between Slieve Corragh and Slieve Commedagh.

Slieve Bearnagh's bulk looms over the Ben Crom reservoir.

The view from the Brandy Pad toward the Ben Crom reservoir and Slieve Bearnagh.

The Hare's Gap is probably the most popular access point into the High Mournes.

The Fairy Glen in Rostrevor – C.S. Lewis is reputed to have drawn inspiration from the landscape around Rostrevor when describing his magical world of Narnia.

Kilkeel is home to the largest fishing fleet in Northern Ireland and is the seafood capital of Mourne.

Greencastle was built to defend the southern approaches to the Earldom of Ulster and was probably the largest Middle Age settlement in Mourne. However, it was Carlingford on the other side of the lough that developed.

Gently sloping foothills leading up to the Western Mournes.

Warrenpoint sits at the top of Carlingford Lough, where it benefited from the coastal trade due to nearby Newry. Its rapid development in the mid nineteenth century was hastened by the opening of a railway which cemented its position as a popular holiday destination.

Major General Robert Ross was born in Rostrevor in 1766. He commanded the successful British forces at the Battle of Bladensburg in the War of 1812 but was killed a few weeks later while advancing on Baltimore. The men under his command erected this 100ft granite obelisk in his memory. A strict disciplinarian he nonetheless inspired fierce loyalty in his men.

Kilbroney Park is a fine parkland in Rostrevor.

Cloughmore (*An Chloch Mhór*, the big stone) is a huge granite erratic that was carried along and deposited by ice during the last period of glaciation. It sits high above Rostrevor and looks out over Carlingford Lough.

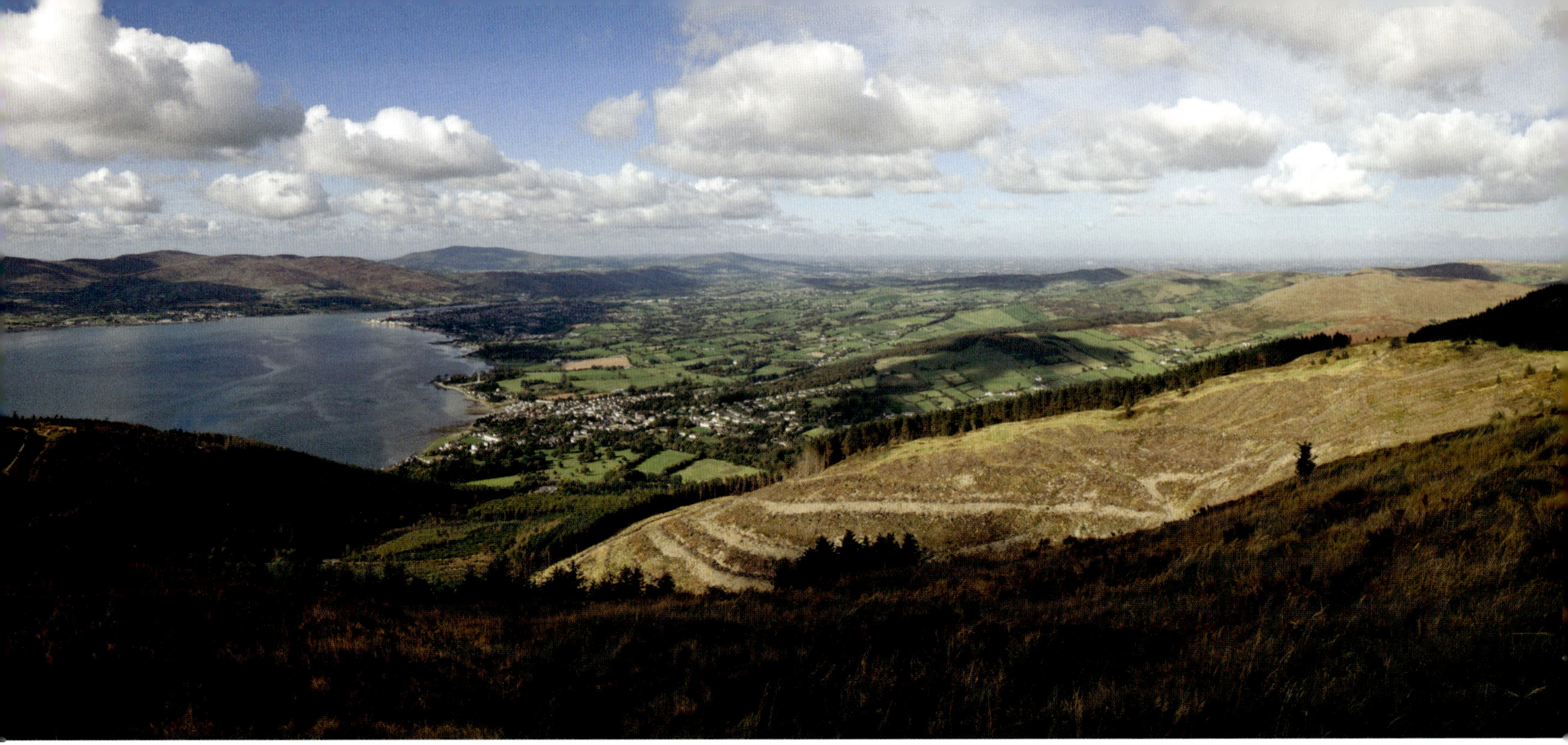

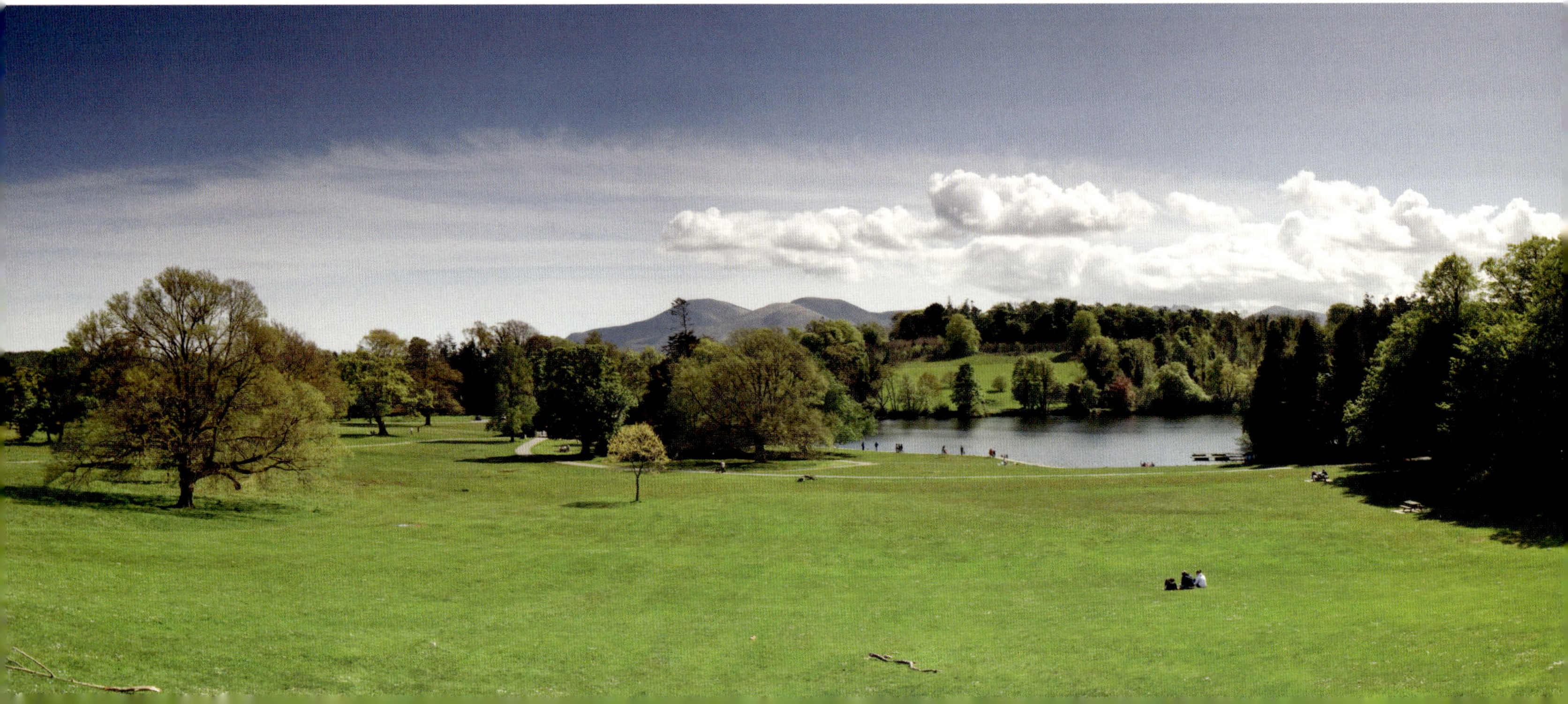

The Kilbroney River flows down through the valley between Hilltown and Rostrevor.

Top left: Looking towards the Newry lowlands from the summit of Slievemartin.

Bottom left: The castle at Castlewellan has a fine view over its parkland and lake towards the mountains.

Inside the High Mournes: Slievnaglogh, Slieve Corragh, Slieve Commedagh, Slieve Donard, Slieve Beg, Cove Mountain and Slievelamagan.

John De Courcy's castle on top of Dundrum Hill was founded in 1177
as part of a series of coastal defences – here controlling access to Lecale.

The Sliderryford Dolmen was one of the sights that travellers on the Belfast to Newcastle railway would crane to see as their train neared its destination.

This mountain ash, below Altataggart Mountain,
appeared to be standing-dead, but still managed to burst into
the seasonal red colours that can be seen throughout the area,
in late summer and early autumn.

The Mournes from Eagle Mountain – the "little peaks" that give
Slieve Binnian its name can be seen dotted along its ridge.

Dundrum across Dundrum Inner Bay. The castle is visible on top of Dundrum Hill.

Early morning mist over the hills around Dundrum.

Carrigs River flows into Dundrum Inner Bay, but despite appearing to come from the direction of the Mourne Mountains, its waters come from Slieve Croob and Cratlieve to the northwest.

Looking southwest from Slieve Bearnagh.

The Annesley mansions are built on the site of several former castles, one of which gave Newcastle its name.

The Fairy Glen near Rostrevor provides some
pleasant riverside walks.

Traditional willow thatching – turf was laid on the wooden frame before the thatching was placed on top. Pine boards would have been fixed to the inside to form a ceiling.

Left: Mourne still has some of its traditional homesteads such as Hanna's Close. This "clachan" is a small cluster of houses that housed an extended family. The doors and inward facing windows were larger than the outward facing windows – this basic defensive construction speaks of the troubled nature of the times in which the clachan was constructed.

The granite from the mountains was fashioned into millstones for use in mills such as the Annalong Cornmill. Constructed in the 1800s it continued to operate until the 1960s becoming one of the last working water mills in Northern Ireland.

The gothic Barbican Gate was built around 1780 as the eastern entrance into the Tollymore demesne.

The Spinkwee River is sometimes also known as the Cascade River because of the dramatic cascades just north of the Altavaddy Bridge.

Right: The Hermitage in Tollymore was built by the 2nd Earl of Clanbrassil as a memorial to his friend, the Marquess of Monthermer.

This elegant footbridge over the mouth of the Shimna was constructed as part
of the regeneration of the promenade in Newcastle.